FISH

RUST FISH

poems

Maya Jewell Zeller

LOST HORSE PRESS
Sandpoint · Idaho

Acknowledgments

I would like to thank the editors of these fine journals, in which some of these poems first appeared:

Blue Collar Review: "Billiard Cloth"
Blue Earth Review: "Skunk Cabbage," "Kelp Noise," "The Rust Fish" (1) & "The Rust Fish" (2)
Camas: "Her Willapa July," "The Rust Fish" (4) & "The Rust Fish" (5)
The Cincinnati Review: "After the Highway Slides Out" & "Chanting the Alders"
Crab Orchard Review: "Catkin," "Marymere Falls," "The Red Room" & "The World at Eleven"
Crowd: "Cousins"
Ecotone: "Socioeconomic"
The Emerson Review: "Foxglove"
Hayden's Ferry Review: "The Person Who Stays Home"
Isotope: "Swing"
Knockout: "Orchards" & "Revenge"
The MacGuffin: "First Friday of Spring"
The Meadow: "Clarissa" & "The Insomniac Speaks in Winter"
Pank: "Beetle Summer," "She Dreams of Being an Artist" & "The Woman Who Bought Our Place by the Ocean Burned It Down"
Phoebe: "The Boy President"
Poet Lore: "Goddammit," "The summer Sky & I made a game of collecting trespasses" & "Tire Hut: Seaview, Washington"
Puffin Circus: "Sandpit" & "That Purple Were the Color of Our Skins"
Rattle: "I Give You Ten Reasons Why We Can't Use Roundup on Our Lawn"
Raven Chronicles: "Migration"
Regarding Arts & Letters: "Sibling Rivalry" & "Saturday Shopping"
Slipstream: "Serape"
South Dakota Review: "Registered Horses"
Southeast Review: "Oyster"
Spoon River Poetry Review: "She Believes She Can Breathe Underwater"
West Branch: "Something Like Singing in the Rain"

The poem "Tire Hut: Seaview, Washington" also appears in the anthology, *New Poets of the American West*.

Additionally, I am grateful to the following friends for their careful reading of these poems: Jonathan Johnson, Christopher Howell, Kathryn Nuernberger, Zachary Vineyard, Jessica Moll, Grace Danborn, Christine Nicolai and Rachel Mehl.

Cover Art: "Reveries," oil on canvas by Mel McCudden, Spokane, Washington
Author Photo: Christopher Zeller
Book & Cover Design by Christine Holbert

FIRST EDITION

This and other fine Lost Horse Press titles may be viewed online at www.losthorsepress.org.

Library of Congress Cataloguing-in-Publication Data
Zeller, Maya Jewell.
Rust fish : poems / by Maya Jewell Zeller.—1st ed.
     p. cm.
ISBN 978-0-9844510-9-8 (alk. paper)
I. Title.
PS3626.E363R87 2011
811'.6—dc22
                                        2011006955

Contents

Oh, summer, my body is open-mouthed like a fish.

—Melissa Kwasny, *Thistle*

Soak the map
in rain and when this cheap dye runs
only glaciers and the river names remain.

—Richard Hugo, *A Run of Jacks*

I

The Rust Fish

leap on their poles, ride sidewalk
toward river. Once they gleamed silver,
glowed bronze in the Bellingham sun,
once they glitzed chrome
under smoke-town moon. People
would come to see their own bright
reflections in the freckled statues,
look into the fishes' eyes and know
what stone to carve their souls from.
Elders burned cedar, fanned smoke
to these fish. Women imagined themselves
sea lions swimming up Whatcom Creek,
swallowing brilliant pieces of gods.

Today a girl leans her bike on this salmon's
red stick, pink plastic streamers
from her handlebars making whiskers
across a stuck jaw. The bugs
aren't afraid; they buzz
and glimmer as if no teeth, no snap
could crush them again.

But tonight when constellations whiten
and bang against black, these fish
leave their rods to the low-lying fog, rise
in long jelly arcs as if no metal
contains them, as if
they might spawn stars.

Skunk Cabbage

Your spiked
flower
hardly knows

its own allure. Like
lemon cookie, like
hooded

clitoris. Shake you
and you let go
dew.

Your name
means dew
in Hebrew,

my mother tells me
at thirteen.
I've spent

the day staring
at skunk
cabbage, rubbing

the stamen
glow
between fingers,

learning
its curve,
and ah!—the pulpy

bumped berries
fleshing
its core. If I

were water
I'd catch
in the cup of you,

swamp lantern,
I'd reside in the light,
the rosette

of your hips.

The Woman Who Bought Our Place by the Ocean Burned It Down

Where the house had been, hot ash
singed the bracken fern. Except it wasn't a house;
it was a gas station, and perhaps

the ferns burned up
too, but there must have been blackberries,
skunk cabbage, ocean spray

with its little foam flowers
hanging like grapes by the chicken coop,
leaves grayed by the smoke

but not ruined. And the apartment up top
had held curtains, a couch. My parents could still see
the shudder of crimson against dusk,

hear the bang of the frame
as it fell. Where was I? Lying like cinder
in the room of my birth?

Perched like a gull in the bathroom
upstairs, rising through the hole in the floor
my father chainsawed to let up the heat?

They stood together that night
holding my young body, listening to the waves,
the loud crack of salt against rock,

the occasional outbreak of wings
scraping black, their nostrils flared
with the confluence of creek to sea.

The Red Room

The fact is, I was a trifle beside myself;
or rather out of myself, as the French would say.

—*Jane Eyre*

What can you do when they lock the door? Pray? Or feel the flame inside the chest, a flicker darking hard its blaze against the ribs' flesh. Your skin cherries as if pricked: there is another you inside the mirror, a spirit-girl with hands of sun and sumac, sharp hands that hold a glowing light. Put your palm to hers, fingertip to blushing fingertip; they ring like bell-tongues meeting metal walls. And this you're sure of: your hands fold together and she leads you through the glass as if stepping past the columns of a waterfall. And here's a boat. You stand unsteady as you sail across a sea of swirling wine, legs slowly jellying, eyes wide as strawberry flowers. Here is a world where you are one of them, where you can know what to say. A world of stone and ocean, coral blooming from the brine like a hungry wound. Like your song, its raw notes salting the wind. You will never have to feel the shame again. These waters course your heart, the throaty cave you'll never want to leave. Never scream. Never thrash against the door. No one need come rushing.

Sandpit

Behind the veggie garden our father made a pit of sand
for us to play in.
                    G.I. Joe lived there; it was the middle east
and he had to keep under the pine twig cave we'd built
or else he'd melt. At any time
green cone bombs might fall or god-kids kick scratchy dirt
into his eyes.
                    G.I. Joe landscaped with pumice, red scoria
and lichen. Sometimes a bluebell or a sprig of sage. He knew
the small things mattered. A touch of green
just peppered in
can brighten up a room.
                    G.I. Joe loved lambsweed with warm
government cheese. Once a week he rode his motorcycle
to the food bank, sidecar full of canvas bags.

The building's logs were thick and brown,
a swing set hung where Mother
told us not to play with kids whose mouths
were framed in dirt. We drove away
with powdered milk and "trash" my mother said
we wouldn't eat: doughnuts, white bread,
colored cereal shaped like Os.
My mom stirred water into milk.

My gums grew numb with clumps of chalky
white, like swallowing quartz-rich sand.

Beetle Summer

The bugs came buzzing black
and red against my attic window.
The ceiling boards were bare and warm.
The air space smelled of pitch,
wet dust, vanilla candle, shingle tar.

My room was raw with its own smallness,
its window-ledge littered with their dead
or writhing bodies. These were not
lady bugs. No wishes, no fly-
aways. Just their ripe crawling,

the heat magnified by their spotty shells,
and to still the rot, to make some breeze,
each back opening and closing on itself,
as if a thousand eyes blinked and drilled, drilled
and drained me with their piercing glow.

Sibling Rivalry

G.I. Joe told Skipper
she'd never be anything
because she was a girl,
then my brother drilled a hole
from her chest to her back
and hung her from the ceiling
of my bedroom so when I walked in
I'd scream.
                        I did scream,
and when I was done
I mutilated Joe
the way a boy tortures beetles
or dismantles toy girls.
                        I can still remember
each tug against the thin, taut
elastic strings, his body making pings
and cracks, black plastic falling
from the shoulders, springs popping
out, one cracked hole
where an arm had been, socket
gaping like a shocked jaw.

The Boy President

When you saw that small boy
down by the railroad tracks bent low,
his whole body focused for once
on some important task, you probably knew
he was lining Lincolnhead pennies
to smash on the iron rails.

In the trees beyond these rails
there's a lidded bucket where the boy keeps maps
to countries he made up in his head. He stores
rusty safety pins, piles of zippers,
and broken light bulbs, filaments filling
a Styrofoam cup. All the glow gone out of them.

But look closer:
it's not coins but crickets he's lashing
to the tracks, their bodies immobile
and bound in blue fishing line,
eyes like tiny moons orbiting a lost planet,
thin copper bodies shining in the dark.

Clarissa

Mean boys teased Clarissa for her smell.
At Clarissa's the potbellied pigs were pets,
cradled or ridden by toddlers.
A chicken strolled across the counter.
Their house hung over the slough,
porch mossy as a tree, until you couldn't tell
that tanned planked deck
from the slow swell
of alder-strewn brown water.

When floods came, they packed their stuff upstairs
and watched old furniture float past.
Clarissa told me she once saw the sofa
she'd been born on,
trapped between pilings a few feet out,
pink begonia print bleeding in the current.
A raccoon was sort of stuck on it, she said.
It was the strangest thing I ever saw.

Revenge

Now this girl is wriggling her fingers between chafe
and chafe of rope, the fine strands curling out
of themselves like tendons unhooking.

She's unpressing her back from the tree bark
where her brother and Billy left her
after promising this time she could play, after leading her

into the woods, shoving her to ponderosa
where her spine learned the deltas of bug-ridden bark
while her brother wrapped twine around and around

to fasten her like an insect for science. Their boy
feet stomped away into sagebrush, laughs cracking
hot air. The girl waited for the last sound

of their leaving. She waited and watched the sky
through spiked needles and rust trunks. She let
her chest collapse into softer breaths,

counted the bluebells nodding to each other,
the chipmunks enlisting, the beetles heaving
from sandy holes. She heard their six-scrape clatter

as they ran from the sun. She let the woody
brushed scent of penstemon inhabit her clothes,
the call of a chickadee raise the hair on her knees.

And now she slips from the cord.

The World at Eleven

The night road is cold beneath us, our jeans
drawing in the damp like sphagnum moss.

It's a back road, and you called me crying again
so I met you here to listen to how your father

and mother let him stay with you, how he entered
your room at night and convinced you to let him sleep

in your bed. It was just last week
you made your fist into a dark hole,

pushed your right index finger through to illustrate
sex. I'd read the books my mother gave me,

and your explanation seemed too simple,
not enough pink and red and purple

pictures. We giggled and lay back on the barn's
spilled hay, watched swallows making a nest above us.

That's what I want my first love to be, I'd said.
Building together a home out of mud.

It was something we both could understand,
your parents and mine neighbors across these silt

flood fields, lights almost visible at night from houses
high enough so rising waters couldn't reach.

In another two years you'll show me
how to use a tampon, laugh at me

for not having kissed even one boy
since you will have slept with three.

For now you put your head to my shoulder
and soak my shirt. You use lines you've heard

on *Guiding Light:* I didn't say no. It hurt,
then he held me. I'm not sure I can go on.

The moon's flat face wavers behind clouds
and trees. I can hear the river moving, so I stroke

your hair, point to the water. Summer's coming, I say.
Tomorrow will happen. That's what time does.

Cousins

We spent all afternoon
running through the muddy rows
of filberts, gathering
the windfall nuts
in a ten-gallon
bucket, cracking their shells
with a hammer
on the grass-split cement
by the basketball hoop,
washing brown casings
from the court with a hose.
In the evening
I'd already had a bath, but the skin
on my soles was creased
from summer running, the callus
of being seven. So Heather
brought a bottle of nail
polish to her room, put me
on the edge of the bed.
She gave me lotion
to rub on each foot, all
my small toes, and uncapped
the red paint.
In her purple
pajamas she was the most gorgeous
girl I had ever seen, her hair
streaked like the light
you can see when you sprint
past an even line
of nut trees in afternoon,
the sun cracked
into a hundred corridors of orange.

The summer Sky and I made a game of collecting trespasses,

we found a noose
hanging from the rafters of that old
abandoned barn. We took turns
standing on tiptoe to slip
our necks through the hole, and I posed
with tongue lolling and rolled eyes
while Sky squared his thumbs
and index fingers to mock a photograph.

How many times
did we think about torching
that old barn down, or the unlocked house
strewn with rain-soaked porn,
as if the renters left
in the middle of sex
or first thing in the morning
after a windstorm?

Outside the sun was shining and we lay,
Sky's head on my belly.
Branches leafed a kaleidoscope
of green and blue.
Sky bounced an apple from palm to air,
palm to air. Then he pulled
a pearled knife from his jeans.
For a moment that blade was beautiful
in the August light, a silver glint
I could see Sky's dark eyes in.
Then quick as a spark
sharp metal met fruit
and pierced straight through its core.

It was the sound of flesh hitting water, a plush

body gone crisp with cold.
Sky passed half to my waiting palm.
We lay there and ate,
teeth cracking through skin,
juice streaming our necks
with its sweetness,
its cool rope of sap.

Cemetery by an Empty Barn

What if this girl has a mouse, white
as the blooms of phlox that spot the clay cliff by her house,
where she takes the mouse and lets it sniff around
while she draws fish with a stick in the clay. This mouse she
calls a mouse, others call a rat. While the girl is sleeping,
her brother takes the mouse, stuffs it in a red
plastic Easter egg, clips it shut, careful not to catch the tail
or whiskers or fur in the crack. He throws the egg
in the air again and again. His sister is dreaming.
She sees the red sphere rise, crack: her white animal
has wings, a horn, a ladder for her to climb. So she climbs.
The mouse flies above her town. She thought the town was so small,
but from above she can see fences past each fence, gardens
past each walled garden. The mouse lands in one of them, crouches low
to the earth. She climbs off its back and sits in a pile of smooth
shells, white as the fur of her mouse who is now
licking and licking the salt of the shells. The shells are singing.
There is a *shh, shh*. There is a rock-rolling-in-water sound,
a persistent thump as if yellow-haired horses might come to leap
the wall. While she watches the gray stone wall of the garden, she cuts
her palm on a shell, stains it red. And she wakes.
She goes down the stairs to find her brother listening to loud music,
and she can't find her mouse, and finally she sees
through the black netting of speaker the red plastic egg,
and it isn't difficult to pull the front off the speaker
while her brother laughs on the couch. Inside
is the egg. She pulls it out and the mouse falls
into her palm, pink feet trembling like the skin
of her hand, mouse tail wound tight, pink eyes wild
and rolling. The next day her mouse dies.
She takes him to the field by the barn
where she buries all the animals who die. She digs alone,
while a crow sits on barn-wire and watches the fields,
watches for brothers with fishing poles. And look:
here is the graveyard, its birch crosses tied together

with morning glory vines. Look: there are crosses for the chicken
she loved, the kitten, the robin she found, its neck bent from a smack
against glass. And listen, she is singing a tune so sweet
you can smell it. The notes are the phlox that grows along clay,
an aria of warm feathers, white fur. And look, animals
now are coming from all around. Walking a spiral. Salt falling
from their tongues, wings, and feet. Garter snakes in the tall grass.
Thrush in the blackberry bush. Deer lifting their heads
from new clover, coyotes dropping their meat. The third verse
of this song is coming. The third verse is important. The ravens
fly down to lift her, to bring her song higher, so even the fish
can feel it rising, shaking their bones in those dark underwater caves.

Saturday Shopping

While my mother searched the stacks
for plates that matched and my sister
plunged through dolls, I renamed
the colors of clothes that lined
the thrift store racks. Black was *outhouse hole*
or *old tire.* The reds ranged
from *dictionary cover* to *hot pepper.*
One divine blouse was *dome of afternoon,*
and I imagined
if I put on this shirt on a blue day
I'd just blend into the sky, match it so perfectly
as I stood hanging sheets on the line
that they'd all have to say,
Maya—Maya—Where did she go?

II

The Rust Fish

are fragile in your sink. You can't
flay them like regular trout,

slide a knife through their bellies
to pull out your next bait.

They'll spear you with millions
of splinters, you'll fear them

for days in your sleep with their teeth
coming at you like blades. Like

the Halloween candy everyone
told you about so you keep instead

in the basement with the lights out
while your parents turn in early,

you listening over and over to the rushing
of steps up your porch,

the knocking like stones to your skull,
feet moving away across your brain,

and the sound of pebbles scraping
the limestone while you wait underwater

never stops, while you wait for these fish
to come alive again, to swim by

and pull you from the bottom
with their sleek rainbow fins, hook you

and tuck you into a gill where you can ride
in an ebb tide to heaven.

Kelp Noise

I kept a stuffed snake
in my bed against Mother's wishes.
She hated that snake,
its four feet of tri-colored fuzz,
the red-white-and-blue of it, striped fur
that turned gray with the grime
of a child. Looped once, twice,
around my leg while I napped, he made me
feel safe. Coiled in ache. Primal as rock.
As if he could mate and make snakes
come alive. When I had mono
Mother threw my snake in the trash,
but I found him, I fished him out,
rubbed dust off his eyes. Let the onyx
beads gaze back at me again and I sang
him a lullaby, *welcome-back, welcome-back*
Snake. That night I walked
to the garden where Mother chopped kelp
into pieces to richen the dirt. Moon gleamed
off the olive skin sheen of the kelp,
flashed blue as the tail of my snake,
crimson like his head and I thought it was him
all bitten in pieces, white polyester
spilling out across beets. I smelled salt-drift
in darkness and knew he'd been packed
with the ocean-foam, knew he had lost
his brine on this plot, lost it to froth
full of bugs sliming dirt and the rubbery
flesh of the kelp-tangled net
and the hole-pocked floats
from boats gone down.

The Accident

When my friend broke her nose
falling off her horse that summer,
the fair was coming up. It must have taken
a lot of courage to go anyway, white
bandage etched against a yellowed
brown, eyes dark and shrunk inside
her face. And I ignored her. Saw her
with her dad and brothers
and walked away. Snaked around a corner
to a bouquet display, orange dahlias
with those flaming sunshine stripes yelling
out their gorgeous song and me suddenly
tasting dust and hay beneath the tables,
my small body shaking and raw.
All around my friend were whipping lights
of Ferris wheels and spinny discs launching
people into space. Could that make up
for pointing children, laughing boys?
She didn't pay me back
the way she should have: punish
me when we got home. Instead
she said I must have been busy, hanging out
with someone else. And later,
when I asked if she could ever be the same,
she said she wasn't sorry
about the fall. She must have learned
to face her life, to know
how she'd have to go it on her own,
know when something throws you into the air
you have to enjoy the arc,
the glowing amber grass beneath,
and when that earth comes rushing
up at you, what else can you do
but meet it head on.

When Wishing Up

I see that summer's tar side
of rafters drip. That hot,
and just the river's keeping cool.
I'm on my back, this barn's hay soft
and sharp at once. Like fourteen.
Plum blossoms. I wanted to be leafed
with you, new green
across our wrists

each day. But then the gray of August sat,
fat as sparrows along tin eaves, their claws
curled tight like sharp fern fronds. I spoke.
I speak. Only the smelt repeat my rasp, their dark
mouths shining awake from alders
strewn white and black against the far clay bank.

Registered Horses

My best friend longed for a Pinto,
which she called a Paint. The difference,
I learned, was a certificate. Her actual horse Misty
was a mixed breed, ruddy brown, dun stripe
like an electric wire down her spine
and we rode her tandem, bareback,
across the floodplain when the grass was tall.
We brought her spotted apples
from the tree by the neighbor's house.

At sixteen we ached to be sultry, our lips
pushed out to pout like Marilyn's in some diner,
James Dean in his black leather washing
our names from his mouth with a vodka. I'd stare
at *Boulevard of Broken Dreams,* which I later learned
was a parody of *Nighthawks.* But back then
why should we care? We still had horses in our eyes,
drove to Tacoma to shop for prom dresses.
Mine was glitzy purple glam slammed to my hips
and when I twisted it turned mermaid green.

The dance had spinny lights and boys,
the after-party beer smelled bad
and I asked Matt to take me home.
While he revved up his Bronco I stood alone
in the dark and heard Misty neighing in her field.
It didn't matter that she had no formal
lineage, no father called Vintage or Maxwell.
She was the real thing,
and I floated like static through mosquito air
to shore up against her hot wet coat.

In the Season of Rivers

We learned to drive on mud
slick roads. Some floods
brought cows across the fields,
carcasses bloating in April sun
until Fitz could get a tractor
through wet ground to lift them.
Our eyes had trouble sticking
to the streets. Beside us trees
were ominous with green;
deep through their branches
blue looked down to streams,
to grass ablaze with yellow blooms.
Our legs ached like horses' legs
ache, not like dormant wheels.

Billiard Cloth

It's not felt.
People like to call it that,
but that's not what we call it.
Felt is mostly cotton,
much less durable, much springier
when pinched between the fingers
and great for Miss Brigg's classroom wall
where you can hang chunks
of barns, fields, black and white
cows which stick
and move across the bright green fabric.

Billiard cloth is seventy percent
wool, at least, and scratchy
with traction. But not sticky. A fraction
of cloth—a long roll—
costs a few hundred dollars
and takes a long time to buy
while you sit and wait
playing cards with your sister
at the warehouse in Portland
where you always stop before a trip.

People say it doesn't matter
what you call it. But
I guarantee if you slip
and miss the cue ball on felt,
you'll tear a hole straight
through to the slate.
Which, by the way, *is* actually
slate, and on some tables, takes three
grown people to lift.

When I think of our van,
it has a bolt

of billiard cloth
splitting its middle like a spine.
Each leftover patch
we put in a bucket.
My mother pieced scraps
for blankets warmer than wool,
itchy to the chin but good for winter
in an old farmhouse on land
we didn't own.

Animal Dreams

Racoon fetches a small white stick and holds it slant. I learn to cast the colors all around my room, to make a watermark of light. We go to the dory in the yard, brush off the piled leaves and flip it to its front. Climb in, he nods and I am sitting in the hull and soon we're floating up the dusty chant of light from my white stick. The light is everywhere now, autumn wisps of ash and maple, oak and loam mixed in. We're above the world, the road below unzipping the valley to show the roots beneath the fields. Each twisty curl a tributary asking me to fly down into it. One braided path calling me like a fish called to spawn. But wait—there's a deer beside that street, and there's my brother's truck and now he's getting out and standing over her, a rock above his head and now he's knocking on her skull as if to see if she will let him in. And now he's hugging her around her neck, and now he's turned it like a skeleton key, and now he's pushed her toward the duckweed in the ditch, and now he's back inside his truck, the smoke so thick I can't quite see.

Chanting the Alders

From these limbs swim smelt,
upriver   easily swimming, the volta
of shadow   calling you back.
Salmon swallow them, throats
sticky with scales. Then sea lions,
each gray-brown speckled body
rubbing its belly up rocks.

You stood on this bridge at fourteen
and heard the water singing
all its terrible songs.
You wanted its stones
on your tongue: the granite,
the siltstone, the greenschist   chafing
your skin buds until you bled green.

What the river said then
stays with you.   It owns you.
Its currents are dark,
waiting in pockets of calm
behind boulders, alders submerged
in the clay bank they sunk with.
They're calling

you under, leaves caught   in the eddies
and flirting each tattered edge
against ebb.
They're calling you.
You.
If only you'd go to them.
If only you'd go.

Serape

On the back deck of my parents' tavern
overhanging the river
I held my sister down, one knee on either side
of her chest
and punched and punched my raw red fists
to her head, her held-out hands,
though I can't recall why I was fighting exactly
and I'm not sure if it was deserved
but I do remember my anger,
the way it stayed with me
all those years even after the bar shut down,
even after that deck eroded into the cutbank,
even when we lived in a new town
and the winter got so cold I gathered all the wool I could find
to wrap around my and my sister's shoulders,
our hands and heads
so that when I pressed my face to the serape our parents
had hung to separate the apartment kitchen
from the billiards room,
my cheek so close the Guatemalan design of red
and yellow bird blended to raw orange in my wet eye,
I could still smell the smoke
of the customers' cigarettes.

Fools' Gold

If you don't grow, you'll rust.

—*Uncle Randy*

Pyrite turns reddish when oxygen
mixes with wet. I was twenty
when I found my first piece, sheer
cleave against cleave, golden
in an outcrop of rock. Mafic.
Hydrothermal calligraphy. Like us,
it is heavy, hard, and fragile,
difficult to value.

At eighteen Randy crossed the equator,
crawled through a tube of trash to prove
how man he was while others banged
their palms against the metal walls
to make them hum. I try to imagine the mold
of thrown-out plum against my cheeks,
ringed plastic rouging marks that won't come off
for days, hot muffled retch of shipmates
worming through in front of me, the taste
of sour puke that makes its way into my throat
despite my melded lips. I can't.

Once I crawled through a tree cast
at Mt. St. Helens, the walls fossiled
with bark-touch. My headlamp's glow
grew weak into the black. I knew the world
was at the other end but shook each time
my knee scraped rock. I couldn't turn around.

After the Highway Slides Out

There's no traffic to make us walk
on the side of the road. Now
we've the yellow lines to pace
as we please,
and our father's tavern closes.

No more tourists asking
which way to the covered bridge,
their new city cars
scaring Joel's horses back from the fence
where they'd come for our petting
and whistle-worn grass blades.

Boys take machetes into their woods
to pile sword ferns thick as meat
on pallets, to sell for three dollars to a man
who drives the long way from Raymond
to pick them up in his blue painted truck.

Or sisters strip
away pieces of white-and-black
bark from cascara

until the trees bleed
orange as the buoys dotting
our flood-fields.

And smelt sells bucket
by silver-limbed bucket
to the men who still somehow come
weekends from Seattle
to fish the lower Columbia
for steelhead and salmon.

All Saturday they sit
in boulder-wedged lawn chairs,
faces toward Astoria,
thinking that smell is the sea,
thinking they might catch
our river on their rods.

Should we show them?
Sealskin spotted with barnacles
slick as peeled daisies
lies rotting on the jagged spit.
The flies buzzing and black
as the pits of your eyes.

She Dreams of Being an Artist

In Brownsmead the house was always cold. I came home from school to sit on the floor and watch deer float from the woods where they froze on the edge of the field and startled the mist. The screen of fog between me and the deer was thick and full of almost-ice. The walls, the floor, the kitchen stove, the paint that spilled onto the windowpane, all a foamy sort of pale. I pushed my lips against the glass, its sharp chill like a pinch against my flesh. I thought perhaps I'd blow into the frost, my warm breath whiting out the world until the window grew hot, my sighs ballooning it out, like artists do in glass shops with colored gobs and iron sticks and fired ovens, until the bubble yawned into the dome of sky, and maybe I could crawl inside that sphere, curl marsupial, the blue coming through becoming green against my skin, morphing yellow, glowing me embryo-orange. Flush of amber, insect trapped inside. This is how my laughing began, how I gasped to hear the scrape of door against its frame and turned to see my mother standing there. My legs were pressed into the cool linoleum, the refrigerator pulsing its current through floor to tickle my skin.

Goddammit

We learn to swear from our fathers
when they're chopping wood
and miss the log,
axe skimming bark
off the woodblock,
dew off the grass,
goddammit raising its hot white streak
into November.

When my father's scanner
picks up police reports,
he's pulling on Key pants,
grabbing black jacket,
out to the garage to pull the tarp
off the tow truck.

I wake to hear the engine
having it out with the cold.
This means potatoes later
for breakfast, fried eggs, bacon
instead of oatmeal.

In my room I want to say it.
The sounds grow lead-heavy
on my tongue awhile
before I spit
out the window.

I shiver awake and worry
about the fate of the woodblock,
the gas stove, the bread knife,
my mother. *It doesn't matter
who god is, or how bad it is to damn it.
If Dad says it,
it's gonna happen.*

Oyster

In my dream of my father I am sitting behind his teeth, his thoughts coming to me through each exhale. He has two full rows of real teeth and he is young. He has stepped outside. Back in the dark his mother is dying, her uterus raw with cancer. My father walks to the park, wants the swings to whisk him into the blue. Before him, girls blush ruddy as pink wool and scatter when he moves. He climbs into the swing, pumps. Soon his legs learn to move on their own, to push him up. Each time he rocks back, the chains stretch taut, and he sees beneath in his shadow an oyster shell wedged in the bark chips. He thinks of the slow agony of oysters, their treasures torn from them, flesh scraped free, shells slowly forming mountains to the stars. My father wants to taste shellfish, to know the slippery smack they make as they slide down a throat. He tips back his head so I have to hang on, opens wide his jaw and I can see the sky, the polished shapes of clouds. His thoughts are hissing by. I can feel the warm jet of breath at my back, lifting me beyond his lips like speech, a name slipped across the palette. This sky is new. This world is open, skittish, and white.

III

The Rust Fish

hasn't slept for days. Weary
of being so ruddy compared
to the other koi, of being
laughed at by children, having rocks
thrown at him, having women
ask their husbands *what's wrong
with that fish?*, he hides under
the waterlily patch by the stone
bridge all day, seeing shadows
of golden and amber and black
and white fish on the gleaming
green bottom of the pond flash by,
waiting for dark when the others sleep
and he breaks through the lilies
to lie on the bridge,
praying the moon to bleach him,
begging the clouds to pass so the light
will enter his bones,
his gills gaping open and shut
in a pink-scarlet flush, eyes
disco flashing
and the rose of his body blooming,
rippling, its sharp spasmic music
finally jerking so much
he has to flip back
into water for breath.

Migration

Come to the sign that says "Seaview, 43 miles."
Roll down your window.
You'll drive the curving delta, where bird and reed
lift together their tremolo to your ear.
Their song disbands the cold. Let yourself
pull over.
                        Behind each rush-clad island,
Chinook pause too, winged fins fanning.

It's not far back to the ocean,
until tide will come to meet the fresh.
A gull turns in the air, your hair tangles itself
across your eyes and around your shoulders,
tangles until there is no getting out the wind.

Her Willapa July

In these hills, you can feel the moon coming up through your feet. Each toe begins to shine inside your boots, and you think you might float away sideways like a water strider on a river bend, all slow and drifty and surrounded in alder catkins which glide the surface around you as swimmy as stars. This is a moon-shining river bend, a boys-don't-know-about-it river bend, the billowy curve of river only she swims in. The moon starts slowly to rock above the tree line, and she puts her toes to the surface edge, makes ripples that echo like moonlight across the sky. Pretty soon she's up to her belly in moonwater, button-to-button with moon-yellow, that moon swinging her hair around like a cat, howling and scratching out notes on the bottle-smooth water, her trying out her own yowl as melody, unsure who dove in first.

As If Darkness Can Mend It All

I thought here I could summon you,
here where the first balsamroot
presents each sage-colored leaf
like an upside-down heart, apex
aimed at the sky.
I thought here I could call you forth,
here where the hills erupt
into a thousand white
and yellow eyes.
I thought here you'd listen
for the trickle of a new spring
spitting from the rocks.
I thought you'd want
to be mist.
But you've gone and found
a new cave.
The truth is you're tired
of all this damn
sunshine, this river
showing off its cheap jewelry,
robinsong, wingflick, white-
tailed deer with their quick tendons,
the new budding spruce,
even fresh bear scat
reminding you
how young you were.

Pull Tabs

In a diary a thin paper strip, and I stare
at a young lime, frozen on a white peel-away pull tab:
I remember being ten when my parents owned a tavern

on a river on a bend in a road where there were no stoplights
no gas stations and no sun. While seagulls flocked
to the river for smelt the fog came in thick. I sat upstairs

in the apartment above the bar, my feet moving
their lazy swish across the squash-yellow shag carpet
to the thump-thump of music from the floor,

the muffled click of cue ball to orange or purple stripe.
I was sure I could smell the strangers' sweat
through the vents, the dusty breath of hops and chips.

My throat was throbbing hum, my fingers one by one
ripping back old pull tabs to expose rows of gold
bars, palm trees, and cherries, their red orb-glow.

Tire Hut: Seaview, Washington

The shop is divided like the brain:
on one side, dull metals lie crooked
like limbs after wind. Men shout things
to each other and no one. Buckets
of bolts line a wall where red and blue
rags hang from nails, already black
with grease. A generator
or tire balancer shakes the floor
as if the ocean were under it pushing
up, and the air tastes like batteries.
This is where the work gets done.
But the customer comes in to wait
on the other side, sees tires splayed out
in pretty black rows. This one for fifty-nine.
This one for seventy. This set on sale:
buy three get the fourth free. Posters of
babies erupting from lying-down tires.
Tables with shiny magazines to lift
and touch, and everywhere
the smell of new coffee, sweet gasoline.
Outside is a half-barrel, steel
or some other metal, rust-colored now.
It catches the rain. My father and brother
keep it there to drown tires in,
to see where the leak is.
The water is the cleanest water
you've ever seen. No kidding.
You can look into that water
and see the mountain from which it came.

Jack-in-the-Box

Port Angeles, WA

For weeks the "Help Wanted" signs
went flapping wildly above the new Jack-in-the-Box
at the corner of Front & Race
while they finished construction
and filled up the space behind the red Formica counter
with my students. When finally
it opened, the daily line of cars wrapping
around the block at lunch
lagged a month or more
and the tardy problem for my fifth period class
required twenty minutes of paperwork
every day after school. Even my brightest
came in fifteen minutes late, chicken
sandwich wedged between lips
which used to come prepared to speak
sparklingly on Flannery O'Connor, Poe.
I longed to hear her questions about gothic
Romanticism, its trace lineage to today, the fashion
we call 'goth' in black and metal trolling the halls.
Why did she go? Soon I began to wonder
what magic this ruby and white burger joint held.
I had no choice. On a Saturday,
I pulled my Dodge in line behind an old brown Ford,
gunrack gleaming through the back window.
I looked toward the strait, its glittering
water sliced aside as the ferry came in.
A horn that cuts fog wailed against my ear until
in front of me a voice called "God Dammit,
even our teacher eats here now."
I looked around and all the heads were leaning
out the windows, eyes stuck on me, as if
Athena herself had materialized in my place.

I could just see through the whipping flags and banners
the sign by Race Street: "Olympic National Park, 3 miles,"
an arrow pointing up.

Something Like Singing in the Rain

I dreamed I was giving birth. It was much easier
than I had expected. The pushing was like playing
an accordion. Or maybe the last three miles
of a marathon. Or being a custodian.
Summers in undergrad I cleaned toilets, dorm rooms
for seven-fourteen an hour. Washed the dust from plastic
fig trees in common rooms while seasonal boarders
played ping-pong or microwaved ramen for lunch,
noodles slimy as organs in a bowl of speckled fluid.
The baby came all at once, like rain in southwest
Washington, like the monsoon that fills cranberry
bogs so the men in rubber boots don't even have to use
the long black hoses set up for harvest. When that rain
comes, we pull over and turn off our music:
it is a no-radio kind of rain. Sometimes it lasts
five minutes; you think the roads might fill up
and the cars float away. You think a seagull might flash
suddenly across the glass. And then the rain stops.
All along the highway cars have their lights on, you can look
and see rows and rows just sitting as if it's the end of the world.
And then one by one they all get back into their lanes,
turn on their radios. The DJs don't even know. They're
miles away in Seattle or Portland where people think
it rains like that but it doesn't. It only rains like that
where cars sometimes get radio and sometimes not.
The baby wasn't crying. It was humming.

Socioeconomic

Silt muscles out the fish, gold tongues of mica
burn between gills. It's because
of flooding. It's because the schools
needed money for books so the county
let logging roar into the hills. Because
men need jobs. Our family used to eat salmon
every Thanksgiving, our plates alive with sky-
pink orange, peppered meat coating our throats.
One year, when homeless Joe
stayed for dinner, he couldn't stop exclaiming
My god this Chinook is good, so good!
As he ate his eyes
were billowed and brown, jaw open
to what might float in. Freckles.
But mostly I recall the hands, big-wind hands,
story-telling hands, their waving like fins
treading water.

The Person Who Stays Home

I'm afraid I've become
one of those people.
You know,
the ones who play Minesweeper
on their computer
instead of reading books
on their days off work,
waiting for something to happen
like the thunking boots of the mailman
to cross the porch, the metal clang
of the black box receiving letters,
or the *Ellen* show to come on,
or for someone to call,
holding the phone on their laps
with the peanut butter toast plate
and the Chapstick so they don't have to get up,
those people for whom
the only disappointment comes
when they click the wrong square by accident,
set the whole screen ablaze
with bombs.

The Insomniac Speaks in Winter

Night is my balcony
where the new sky
drips as it will drip
the rest of my life but not
the way it used to pull soft from itself
and wrap me like a scarf.
Twenty seven years
I've slept lighter and lighter.
The nasturtiums are still brown
with winter.
Winter
still holds the tulip bulbs
and keeps the garden dirt
soft and sodden,
but the clod in my chest
is heavier than this
because last summer's drowsy nodding
was cut away
with the cherry tomatoes,
the yellow beans,
with the last roots pulled
and chopped for compost.
Tomorrow my love will hold me
and show me the orange
glow of morning,
show me the sungleam
sparking the river.
I think that I will want
to go there
and walk into those waters
where trout float like bees from the darkness.

She Believes She Can Breathe Underwater

My brother snaps the rod behind him, then he casts. I'm lying belly-down on the gravel bar, face so close to the shallows my freckles' reflections could be pebbles. Shadow, light. Shadow, light. The current dents and ripples like a candle lit by sky. Trout have fins that flip through pounding winds and so could I. In a damp place I shrink vein-like into a fine boned Pisces, turn my head to find my body an amphitheater of gray. Scales chafe water where my flesh was pink. My feet are fused to a tail that whips its tinny ping into the rush. I am swimming. Raw river siphons through my gills, air catches in the net of me. There was a time you could have flashed a silver hook into my face, a time I'd jump for whir of wing or trickled green. I'm going to stay here now, where the weeds sway a little with the hum, where the world is safe behind a wet, unbreakable mirror.

IV

The Rust Fish

will never leave this shale.
Here they swim to the future
while palm fronds gesture
them forward. Tourists gape
and wonder, snap their fingers,
wish they could climb rock
with axes to take these bones home.
The fish are indifferent, skeletal
and staring in photos. How many millions
of years ago were they down there
in the bay, their slimy bodies
still pulsing with tides, their eyes
aware of light and dark,
mouths open and tasting
like children's.

Foxglove

Again I run these hills to find
you, bells of anger. Each bloom
where once a hemlock stood.

I used to call it bleeding,
but the cuts were so sweet. I pulled
your coned tubes one by one

and placed each base between
my teeth, the tip a straw.
I drank like bees drink, giddy and high.

Sing pink, I'd hum. Sing your licked
petals, your wet rimmed whistle
like bottles left to wind.

Buzzing shook your faces.
My lips glazed numb
with fuzz, my tongue funk-electric.

I didn't need a reason. Curious
swish of flower to wrist,
freckled lips open against blue sky.

Now, your white-splashed necks
nod fuchsia in an early sun.
You trumpet out my ache,

then catch my shaking fingers
in your furry stalks.
From here I see the river still zags

our valley. Zips it like an s-curve spine.
I used to pray you'd fold
into the breeze, grown bold

by your own bad fairies. Take
me with you, I'd say, sail me
until I tingle green as drooped wool.

Would it have changed
if I knew what I learned later,
how poisonous you are,

how your beauty could burn
my muscle tissue,
choke my circulation?

Again your voice rises.
I take you whole, the purple of you
already in my throat.

For a Student Come Back from the Quiet Beyond

One Sunday morning she calls laughing
from the borrowed truck they've parked
outside my house, having driven eight hours
from the other side of the state to see me.
Her black kitten Hercules is leashed
to the rainbow belt which holds up her jeans,
army coat and the same sleeveless shirt
with a laughing clown she's had since high school.
She's still too skinny, though she tells me
she's been eating granola, yogurt, taking
her multivitamins. While her girlfriend
walks the cat in the pines we go for a run
to catch up. I hear about the years
since I've seen her last: the months
working in a Bahai camp kitchen,
peeling potatoes for a woman who never noticed
the scars, the blue of her heart-beating veins
beneath an arm smudged black with grease.
Then time spent homeless in Seattle,
trying out drugs and different ways to sleep.
Once she sat in the back row
and wrote stories, wanted
to form a writers group her senior year
and joined cross country to travel the state.
She is the student who made me cry the most.
She loves her job at a dry-cleaner's
where the chemicals give her hives
but her boss says she's the best employee
he's ever had. *How can you live here?*
she asks me. *It's so cold. There's too much ice.*

First Friday of Spring

This evening I cut your hair
in the kitchen while we listen
to Bob Seger tell us
it's funny how the night moves.
I could sing along, add
a bar or two about the way dark
brings its heavy water
against my bones like lake
to driftwood. Today we walked
a rim of indigo
and counted the subalpine buttercup,
the first stars of Idaho blue-eyed grass.
My hands slide through the light
brown of your now-short hair,
finding your skin
like fingers sinking to reach
new sand. This
is my favorite part, your breath damp
through my shirt,
your eyes an open sea
calling me in.

Neighborhood Kids

I've got the hose aimed at the yellow beans
when they come up to the fence, hands

gray with August dust, eyes sun-wet
from their latest game of chase. Pumpkins!

they shout, and want to know can they have
this one that's grown beyond

the metal diamond links into Ella's yard.
I tell them it's not ready yet.

One boy with a red plastic bat asks
do I have any fruit. Well, I have cherry

tomatoes, I tell him, and yes, he can have some,
so I bring him a handful. Another pair

of kids show up, can we have tomatoes too,
and I'm thrilled they want to eat them,

feeling smug about my garden and its effects
on their immune systems, how they'll all

grow up to be vegetarians and save the planet,
be the next Clinton or Carter or Susan Sarandon,

champion solutions to the urban feral cat problems,
because today they encountered home-grown food.

Someone's little sister arrives, her hands
cupped, and I ask wow have you guys eaten all

the other ones already? Oh, they're not eating
them, she tells me. They're hitting them with the bat.

Note

Beneath this chicory
sky, bare
arms wrap air inside themselves.

Whistle-worn grass blades
stain teeth
green as my sleeves.

I know all there is to know
of feathers,
all of wings made from apple leaves.

Creek water's cold eddies over
toes, this white
skin running pink as a feldspar vein.

All right, all right. It's true:
all I can feel
is the last place you kissed me.

Catkin

We all know there was a snake. A snake
in a tree in a wood where a woman was waiting
to make a mistake. But it wasn't a snake.
When the cougar opened its mouth,
a pearl the size of a plum sat curled
on its tongue. A gray pearl, fuzz-
covered, like a catkin sleeping. And it leapt
from the tongue to a leaf, to see the dark
and pale sides switch
back and forth, to see light bounce
down the bark. This
was the woman's favorite tree,
her thinking-alone tree.
When she arrived she saw the kitten
and picked it up by the scruff of its neck.
She brought it to her breast, because she thought
it was hungry. It drank while the woman swayed
the way wind rocks a leaf in its sleep,
tugs it to come into the blue. She rocked him
until he was a human child. The sky was dark.
The tree hummed with bees
bedding down. The woman sat at the base
of the tree, which was not an apple
but a plum, and she picked some
and let the juice run down her chest. The baby
licked his lips in his sleep. He brought her fingers
into his mouth. The juice was sweet,
the way women and babies sleep.
The moss was soft like a bed faraway
where a man and a woman
eat plums. The juice was dark
like a sky in a wood. By the tree
while the woman and child
slept, mist crept like a snake and wound
round their limbs, around their bed-soft moss,

and the earth smelled of ferns waking up,
old trees and damp clay.
When the man found them sleeping
so still, he thought she was dead.
His heart swelled like a plum and grew dark.
He stamped, thought the mist was a snake
that had strangled his wife,
pulled a rock from the earth
and chopped at the tree,
at the mist, at the moss.
Heat swelled his tongue to the size
of a plum, the insects asleep
in his teeth shook awake,
flew out where compared to that sky
the child looked bright as a catkin
or plum blossom, curled filled with nectar
to drink and make honey drip from,
and they went to drink, to have plum-sweet
honey, hot between the teeth.
But the child was not a flower. The bees
grew angry, bodies humming with sleep.
They stung and stung until the boy
lay dead, head limp as a limb hung
with honey. All the while the woman slept.
The sky was dark.
The man saw what he had done.
He carried her back to her bed in the ferns
by the creek where yesterday they'd played
frond games with the still-curled green,
where they'd talked of the light and dark
in the water. When the woman woke,
she didn't remember. She didn't remember.

Marymere Falls

You stand on the ledge across from it,
both hands in your pockets.
The dew on your hair
is clear as ice.
Listen: It can be simple.
This water will fall
wherever it wants to,
moss springing
like birds from its spray.
There's nothing you can do about it.
It doesn't even know you're here.

I Give You Ten Reasons Why
We Can't Use Roundup on Our Lawn

1. As a girl the black-branched plums
behind the far fence were mine because
a giant row of nettle and snowberry
blocked them from the cows. I'd lie in a crook
where many limbs came together
and move my tongue along the sticky tip
of a still-hanging fruit.

2. My palms have been stained
again and again
ripe blackberry pink.
I've pressed them to T-shirts
like silk-screened bleeding hearts.

3. Your Jesus
is thin, his eyes dark like lake.
He is hungry. Maybe he'll drink
the milk from these slim green necks.

4. Barbed Wire and Roundup were both
bastard sons of Zeus. They were banished
to America because, as the god himself put it,
they didn't seem to have any *real*
mythical potential.

5. Maybe the grass
is a weed. Then what do you exterminate?

6. My first dream of you
was while lying in a field of golden stems.

7. I don't know how to separate my love
into categorical pros and cons.

8. The lefternmost puff of yellow lies
less than seven feet from where I want
to plant my tomatoes.

9. The back of the bottle reads:
TOXIC. KEEP AWAY
FROM CHILDREN.

10. When you say you want to kill
the dandelions, I cringe.
Plum limbs crack
against the petalled night. Thistles
turn their lavender heads like girls,
whiten and blow cold.
In your eyes I see sprinkler system
installation, stained deck, a mother
in ironed beige pants. Imagine
growing up wild, I say. Lambsweed
is dinner. Pumpkins make bread.
Nasturtiums are honest-faced, edible, and paint
a salad to resemble the sun. Don't you want
to kneel wet-kneed in this green,
bend close to this yellow flower,
press your lips to it, and pretend
you're kissing me?

Swing

During floods Grays River swelled brown
and brought things from other farms, the ocean.
Then the fields were gardens
of logs, rope, wire, and laid-down grass.
My brother pulled a still-wet buoy,
an orange teardrop with blue on top
from a tangled net, anchored it
to a rafter with thick barn rope.
I'd lob one stringy leg on each side
of the tied knot, hang on, launch
from the highest bales and swing
pendulum-like over the flung hay,
the barn floor silt. Head tipped
back. An upside-down world. I ached
for the wonderful *woosh!* it made, the drop
in my stomach, the red chafe on my palms
where frayed rope rubbed, the lurch
as rafters came close on the swinging-out side,
the sail at blue where the tin door jawed open
and the swallow-cries circled my ears.
My friends took out the *u,*
said I had a boy between my legs.
But it was more than something dirty
on the tongue. I *was* the freshet—
moving as inanimates do,
no intended direction, no dodging design,
my arms tucked in with the current, my body dipping
up-down, up-down, my roots ripped quick
from the cutbank, a luck as free
as the willows washed loose by deluge.

Orchards

How tired I am of telling my story,
of pushing it again and again
into words.

Telling how I spent so much time
leaning against the cool words
on gravestones.

I liked that people had lives
and I didn't have to listen. Instead,
I could plant my cheek to their buttercup

carpets, their fern limbs,
each slab rising like a cold tree
from the sloped green.

Like the orchard
where I rode my bike
to walk the hills and stream and pretend

I owned the place. No one
was ever there. No one ever said
You can't. The current of blossoms

smoothed my arms as I passed.
The home it was
when we weren't moving.

About the memory I don't know how to place:
my father, walking through apple trees,
a low fog covering his face.

Did we pull off the road
to pick fruit? Somewhere a bird is calling.
I look at my feet: flattened grass, a broken shell

of robin's egg. I look up:
my father's eyes through the gray.
What blue.

That Purple Were the Color of Our Skins

How tender our names are.
Children bruise them
all our young lives,
until they grow thick
with the ache.
We hold them out
for ridicule, membranes
we sacrifice. Or prune
them back,
disguise ourselves
from ourselves.
Or hide them
under thick cloaks
of other names.

To be like the thistle,
its thorns invisible
until one picks it,
its furry flower like a bee's
back, beautiful and shaking
its warning at us.
And when it decides
it's all over,
that the air is too cold
and strange fingers
have grown too familiar,
it just turns white
and leaves its body
altogether.

The Rust Fish

has had enough now. It's time
you all go home; he's tired
and needs some water. See
how his eyes let their pink show
between cheek and lid. Hear
that rasp as he tries to read you
one more story. You know
he'll keep going like this
if we let him, rocking
in that chair in the corner
of the library, slow voice
drowning his own dry ache,
young ones minnowing
the rug beneath him,
words brining the air like salt.

Notes

This book's first epigraph is from Melissa Kwasny's poem "Nettles." The second epigraph is excerpted from Richard Hugo's "A Map of the Peninsula."

"The World at Eleven," page 12, is for Jessica.

"Cemetery by an Empty Barn," page 17, is influenced by the work of Brigit Pegeen Kelly.

"The Accident," page 25, is after Dorianne Laux's poem "The Job" from her book *What We Carry.*

"Registered Horses," page 27, is for Shana.

In regards to "The Rust Fish," page 59: On Chuckanut Drive, just a few miles south of Bellingham, there is a place along the road where you can see gigantic palm fossils in the sandstone.

"For a Student Come Back from the Quiet Beyond," page 62, is for Mell.